Next Level Sales

A GUIDE TO FINANCIAL AND PERSONAL SUCCESS AND THE MILLION DOLLAR LETTER

Michael Lehman
#Master Your Craft

Clovercroft Publishing

Next Level Sales: A Guide to Financial and Personal Success
and the Million Dollar Letter

© 2021 by Michael Lehman

Published by Clovercroft Publishing, Franklin, Tennessee

Published in association with Larry Carpenter
of Christian Book Services, LLC
www.christianbookservices.com

Edited by David Brown

Cover and Interior Layout Design by Suzanne Lawing

Printed in the United States of America

978-1-954437-14-2

No one answers
the phone anymore.
It's just too easy not to!

Hardship can lead to complete failure or absolute victory. I could have easily given up, but I genuinely believe that success comes from hard work, determination, and ingenuity.

This story starts in the most uncomfortable financial position I have ever been in. One day, I arrived at my job as a Honda sales consultant, distracted and concerned, as a tow truck pulled up close behind—trying to repossess my truck. My mortgage had not been paid in a year and my electricity was about to be turned off. For the first time in my life, I borrowed money from a friend. This $200 loan would be my incentive to move forward and find freedom in financial independence.

The day that I decided to take control of my financial situation changed my life. I set an ambitious objective that would require a creative plan and solid motivation to achieve it; I would earn Honda Gold Master status. I would never again let an impermanent obstacle stand in my way.

Since potential customers were no longer taking my phone calls, there had to be another way to reach them. I developed a long-term strategy. I approached my GM and explained my plan: to connect with prospective buyers, I was going to send birthday cards to everyone I could for the next few years. I realized very quickly that this extra effort was paying off. As potential customers stopped by the Honda dealership, they smiled and thanked me for their cards! I decided to step up my game and began sending out cards with the intent to purchase vehicles. I bought inexpensive blank cards and wrote the message: I WANT TO BUY YOUR _____ in green sharpie. I began sending out ten to fifteen a day, resulting in hundreds of cards containing my name and contact information reaching potential customers within the month. Customers started calling ME instead of hanging up when I called them. When my phone rang, I informed clients that I had a buyer for their vehicle. The increase in customer contact led to an upsurge in sales and an obvious increase in income. My goals were materializing!

Follow my lead. Take the initiative, seize opportunity, and be persistent. There is more than one way to accomplish a goal—adjust and adapt to the circumstances! Remember, you are either riding life's roller coaster or you are running your life's business!

Outside, 80 percent Chance
of not Selling.
Inside, 50 percent Chance
of not Selling.
Sitting them at your desk, 25
percent Chance of not Selling.
WHAT'S YOUR CHOICE?!

Want to be a top performer?

Wanting to be a top performer is going to be extremely easy. Why? Because of the 80/20 rule. The 80/20 rule maintains that 80 percent of outcomes (outputs) come from 20 percent of factors that will produce the best results. So if you pick a dealership with thirty salesmen, you only have to beat six of them to be the best. That's right! To be the top performer at a thirty salesmen store, you only have to be number one of the six guys. Luckily, around the country, the average is twenty, so you only have to be number one over four guys. Yes, a lot will get you lucky sometimes.

Remember, set your goal at the first of the month, whether it be twenty or thirty cars. You count up on the fifteenth of the month, and you start to count down! What exactly do I mean by count up? So count your cars from the first until the fifteenth. If your goal was twenty-five and you have fifteen on the fifteenth, start counting down the ten. It's possible to sell twenty or thirty on the first of the month, but the psychological part of this on the fifteenth is that you cannot do twenty

…. so count down **ten-nine-eight-seven-six-five-four** *and so on!*

The double-digit numbers are what I call kryptonite. That's right! Salesmen get lazy once they reach ten cars. This is where you pour it on just like a horse race breaks out the gate. Don't be like most salesmen who just come to work every day unemployed. Set a goal that's obtainable. Set a goal that can be tracked on a daily basis, and you will be the number one salesman in the store, earning $200,000 to $300,000 a year. Overcome the kryptonite and you will become Superman.

Living inside the box,
you can't read the label.
You must be willing to step
outside and do what others
wouldn't do.

MENTAL AND PHYSICAL SACRIFICE

Mental and physical sacrifices are essential aspects of a highly focused, dedicated salesperson. It is especially vital that you are mentally and physically resilient in this business. You will have to figure out a way to create strength in those areas while minimizing the negativity that impacts successful salespeople.

Years ago, I remember walking onto the sales floor of a Nissan dealership and being greeted by the sales manager. "Mr. Lehman, we are so glad to have you on our floor! Come down here and let's go sit at your desk!" When we got there, he kicked the desk. I didn't understand why until a salesman crawled out from behind the desk. I use the term "salesman" lightly, as this person was what I call a crackhead! The mental and physical pressure of this business had gotten to this man, so much so that he was doing crack daily and sleeping under his desk, all while maintaining a position at the dealership! This floored me, but I had no idea what I was in for. This corrupt manager allowed cocaine parties to take place at the dealership! He seemed to think this was normal and had ultimately put together a sales group that was either high or drunk most of the time, while on test drives.

Now, here's where focus comes into play; my intention was to maintain true professionalism in the center of all this chaos. I worked from 8:00 a.m. when the store opened until 9:00 p.m. when the store closed, seven days a week. I was a threat to these individuals because I had goals and could not be persuaded to fall into their habits. My co-workers were not motivated; they were simply getting by. They saw me as an obstacle impeding their current way of life. We were required to purchase our own computers, so they would smash my monitors and keyboards. They would tear down my signs and mess up my desk. They tried everything they could think of to make me quit. I even called the local police department three times to try to put a stop to the vandalism. They were not in their right minds and were not deterred by the police.

I worked hard for a few more months as everyone watched. It was genuinely like the *Jordan Effect*, a term used to describe those who keep 100 percent of their focus on what they can control, gaining respect and admiration from others. When Michael Jordan walked onto the floor at a basketball game, the audience, coaches, and other players knew he was about to impress them with his skill, determination, and personality. I aimed to mesmerize everybody in my profession just like Michael Jordan. I also realized it is often necessary to make and keep your friends outside of the business.

I found that the long hours alone will put wear and tear on your body; it is important to maintain a healthy diet and active lifestyle. In this profession, others are typically consuming junk food and energy drinks to jack themselves up, causing health issues and lack of focus! A balanced diet will provide endurance; maybe, try meal prepping for convenience. Another way to strengthen physical health is to work out regularly, whether it is lifting weights, riding bikes, or taking walks. The adrenaline and endorphin rush from physical activity will help you keep your health, your sanity, and your mental game strong. Remember, it is often those closest to you who try to bring you down. Co-workers and managers often play mental games to try to keep you at their level. Improving your mental and physical ability to move forward is extremely important when you have goals to reach. Remember, focus—process—progress.

With time, persistence, and consistency, you will earn respect and others will leave you alone! You must remember, no one has power over you. Maintain your professional focus; realize there are mental and physical sacrifices to be made, and power through until you are proud!

The harder you work to create success, the easier it becomes to find it. I decided long ago that I was going to be successful in my career, which made me very aware of all my surroundings, including obstacles, responsibilities, initiatives, and goals. I also realized that opportunities are always present for those willing to focus on the positive aspects of each circumstance.

One night, after having a few beers, a friend of mine and I headed back to my house. As we pulled in, we noticed my paraglider in the garage. My love for aviation outweighed my restraint as I started the paraglider inside the garage to show my friend how it works. Without realizing what was happening, three hundred RPMs of thrust pushed the propeller and it exploded across my chest and arm. I remember feeling like I was sinking into a pool as the blood flowed through the gashes. It was strange because I wasn't scared and felt no pain. Adrenaline had kicked in as I grabbed a towel and drove myself to the hospital. By 2 a.m., they had sewn me up with eighty-four stitches and wrapped me in bandages. My love for my job and dedication to my obligations motivated me to make it to my sales meeting by 8 a.m. that morning!

A few years later, my chimney cover, which is made of concrete, snapped in half. I climbed up on the roof to take it down. I threw the broken concrete off the roof and went to the edge of the room to climb down the ladder. Somehow, the ladder grabbed my foot and pulled me down fourteen feet. I fell on my left foot, shattering every bone, and watched helplessly as my left foot immediately swelled up. I asked my wife, "How am I going to work?" She had faith and told me it would be okay. I was beyond blessed that since she is employed in the medical field, the doctor she works for met us at the office after hours, took care of me, and wrapped my foot in a boot. Once again, my love for my job brought me to work the next day. Incredibly, my sales manager was planning to have knee surgery and had just bought a scooter that I borrowed for two months because I was unable to walk. It turned out to be the best two months of my career!

The COVID-19 pandemic brought unprecedented challenges in the field of sales. Over 150 individuals were employed at the dealership. One by one, they were regrettably exposed to the deadly virus and tested positive. The most traumatizing part was the fear of the unknown, which was made worse by false information and rumors spread by various media. After I tested positive, I suffered far less than many others. I got a stuffy nose and couldn't taste for around three weeks. That was about the extent of it, although I was exhausted for three months and could not keep up with my normal workout routine. I still managed to make it to work eight to ten hours a day, seven days a week. That trying time was one of my most profitable.

Through all these experiences came some of the best months in the car sales business. I believe this was possible because of my positive mindset and unstoppable ambition.

Loving your job truly means that no matter the sacrifice, you are present and determined to get your job done. If you love your job, then you'll never work a day in your life!

I call it the soft touch,
but a thank you card means
more than you'll ever know
to the customers you now
consider family.

Always write in green sharpie.

America's economy is fundamentally driven by the car business and the medical field. These two industries offer security and success even in the chaotic uncertainly brought on by a global pandemic. Without skipping a beat, the car business and the medical field adjusted quickly to meet necessary safety standards and precautions. The ability to adapt so rapidly and effectively is the definition of intelligence! Even with my extreme drive, I fell backward into a hole. My focus had been broken by the pandemic. As I sat on the couch crying one evening, I realized that this virus had interrupted my process and cut off my progress! Once I pulled my head out of my ass, I developed a custom correspondence called *The Soft Touch*. One was captioned "I hope all is well!" This letter revealed true sympathy and empathy toward my customers, my guests, and my family. After I acknowledged the difficulties of the pandemic and expressed my sincere hopes that all their loved ones were well, I advised them that because of three simple aspects of present circumstances, it was time to buy!

1. Banks were deferring payments.

2. Rates were lower than ever.

3. Savings would exceed thousands over the term of the loan.

I adjusted my delivery method to an email platform and stayed up until 1 a.m. for weeks sending this letter out to everyone on my client contact list! Within a week of unprecedented global financial losses and thousands of people suffering and dying from COVID-19 throughout the world, my business was back to normal with appointments set daily! My personal correspondences had worked. I had taken the time to identify the problem and offer a solution for family members (customers). I made sure I prepared for limited contact in a quarantined environment. With contactless business interaction being the new normal, I lined my desk up with hand sanitizer, disinfectant, Lysol spray, and cleaning wipes and had masks and gloves readily available. This gave customers a sense of comfort and safety as they purchased their new car. Quickly adjusting to "no touch" deliveries, customers were the first to put their DNA on their new vehicles! This was a job well done. I was back on my game. Time for a pat on the back. "Great job, Lehman!" I said to myself! Now, let's move forward and live safely and successfully in this new vulnerable world...

Think of yourself as a
five-star restaurant.
You're serving steaks,
not hot dogs.
Get your customers to sit and
relax in comfort. This will
lower their blood pressure.

A missed phone call is a missed opportunity for the seller and the buyer.

No one answers the phone anymore!

Technology provides ease of communication. We can simply share a destination versus wrestling trying to unfold a map. We can give a quick "yes" or "no" to any question asked with one thumb and a click. We can send a photo across the globe in a split second. Convenience is highly sought after in a society that simply has no time—a society where we grab our meals through a tiny window and pride ourselves on Insta Products.

Does convenience have its perks? Yes! But it almost always removes the element of relationship. Buzzing through life in search of instant gratification leaves us disconnected and isolated from others—especially in business.

The drive-thru barista only cares about turning over coffees until her shift is over and she can go home. She's not interested in how Kevin likes his cappuccino or that Mr. Edwards comes in every day just after 8 a.m. to pick up a coffee for his elderly mother. For one, this is a job. The other understands personal connections to people creates careers—successful, rewarding careers.

The key is relationships. Doing the extraordinary makes a huge difference in the minds and behaviors of your customer—especially in a business like yours.

Let's face it. People do not get excited about the idea of buying a car. Having a new car is exciting, yes. Enduring the painstaking experience of shopping, haggling, filling out the paperwork, waiting, and most times, starting all over again is not anyone's idea of fun. But you can change all of that.

People do get excited about engaging with someone they like—someone who makes them feel good, appreciated, and comfortable. This is why you've got to be more than just a salesman in a tie. You must build relationships, and one great way is to do the unexpected—pick up your phone.

Don't do what's easy. Don't even do what's expected. Give your customer something real when they call. A sincere "Good afternoon" goes a long way and always beats forcing your customer to leave a message. They want to hear you, not a robot or automated recording. They have questions they want answered now and concerns they need addressed today. Give them that.

When they know you are there for them, they become more than a simple customer—they become a friend, and everyone loves doing business with a friend they know, like, and trust.

If you can't invest in the effort to answer a call, your customer will never buy into the idea you will give them any effort after the purchase when they need you the most.

Unavailable

The reality is that an unanswered phone call is a missed opportunity for those actively employed in sales. Social paradigms have changed as technology has developed, drastically altering behavior and communication. With the ability to correspond immediately through social media, standard email, and instant messaging, most individuals appear to prefer the autonomy of written exchanges. The accessibility of these technological tools or amenities offers users direct information, sharing or requests through immediate delivery capabilities along with rapid feedback or results, all within their own time restraints.

Predictably, chaotic schedules and preoccupied itineraries often render calls unanswered because they are either unnoticed or unwanted. The modern glorification of a busy lifestyle has people on the go and simply unwilling to pause for a phone call or a potential interruption that they did not initiate. While a phone call previously signified a friendly conversation, opportunity, or consultation, it now seemingly represents an unwelcome want or need from the caller. Among the various explanations for avoiding live conversations, feeling either anxious or interrupted are predominantly common, while the risk of fraudulent scams adds to their apprehension. First, anxiety can affect individuals in diverse ways. They may dread speaking candidly to another person for fear of sounding awkward or inept. They may have an inability to effectively verbally convey what they are thinking. Or they may have underlying stress caused by multitasking or overworking.

Furthermore, invasive distractions like unsolicited phone calls can disrupt productivity, interfere with organization, and disturb thought processes. These unintentional issues can cause call recipients to feel unprepared and inconvenienced, reducing a caller's probability of an answer. Lastly, although unethical, experienced scammers can exploit vulnerabilities, drain bank accounts, and steal identities, the alarming and growing tendency of criminal phone scams has become dangerous and widespread. These reasons, among many others, consistently prevent cautious call recipients from answering live calls.

Simply stated, there are countless obstacles and complications surrounding traditional phone communication that negatively affect wholesome business and sales efforts. The prospect of connecting with potential clients through customer call lists, cold calling, or other means is truly uncertain, but not impossible.

New methods of interacting with contacts through objective, well-meaning, and personal contextual scripts are essential for advantageous business practices.

CARDS AND LETTERS

Cards and letters have evolved from a humble means of communicating personal or financial information to a valuable, professional marketing tool intended to promote profitable return business and maintain a positive position in the forefront of customers' minds. The first couriers, over 9,500 years ago, delivered clay tokens representative of proposed deals between buyers and sellers. Today, written messages have the power to create unprecedented business and success as well as support professional and personal contacts within an industry.

While ongoing communication can be time consuming and challenging, the benefits of developing long-term business relationships through simple, yet effective cards and letters are well worth the effort. A sincere message to potential or previous customers establishes a salesperson's authenticity and integrity. Customers will recognize that you took time out of your schedule to contact them, demonstrating that you value and appreciate them as clients and friends. By acknowledging milestones or situations within a customer's life, whether it is the joyful purchase of a new vehicle or the chaos of a global pandemic, these messages indicate your true interest in their circumstances and build a connection that creates loyal, repeat customers. A successful and effective message to a customer includes a heartfelt greeting, an informational section, and a reminder that they are appreciated! When both the buyer and the seller profit from a mutually beneficial sale, it's a job well done.

If you ask a salesman,
"How is business?" and he says,
"Slow," then you have a
bad salesman.
**SALESMEN
MAKE THEIR
OWN ECONOMY.**

Why Sell?

In a fully functional society, if you can sell, you have the ability to cut through obstacles of class, status, or upbringing in an otherwise inconceivable way. Great salesmen need no other prop but themselves in order to succeed. Therefore, selling well is a reflection of healthy personal character. In being able to successfully execute the sale, you are demonstrating that you are the type of person who others are drawn to—hardworking and trustworthy—and you are more apt than others to succeed at anything you set out to do.

With that being said, sales is a challenging field to choose to be in. Customers are usually going to greet you in one of two ways. On occasion, you will get those who come in ready to buy, having already done the research and made the choice without the need for your persuasion. The most common scenario, though, is the one in which "I'm not here to buy" is heard throughout the encounter. In all honesty, I prefer this situation. In this instance, my response would be a takeaway. If I am acting as a source of information regarding the product, the pressure is off the customer and there is little to no room for rejection. What most people end up forgetting is that, quite simply, the sale itself does not actually begin until the customer says "yes." Each and every opportunity is a chance for me to both inform and enlighten all while gaining a new customer who I can truly call a friend.

There are only
Leaders and Followers.
Choose well

Leadership is an action, not a position

"Some are born leaders, some achieve leadership, and some have leadership thrust upon them." This intriguing quote by CEO Maurice Flanagan often precedes the question, "Where do you fall in?"

Here's the hard truth—leaders are born. Yes, their potential and leadership symptoms may take time (sometimes decades) to evolve, but it's either in you or it's not.

The problem is too many people equate leadership to promotion, titles, or income. Sally was promoted at her company, so Sally must be a leader, right? Perhaps. Or, maybe Sally was willing to accept the responsibilities, pay grade, or extended work hours when no one else would. Maybe Sally's promotion was a result of recognition for longevity in her position or the most sales in a calendar year. It's also likely Sally will be burned out in due time.

Leaders—true leaders—exemplify leadership traits and characteristics, whether it's their first day on the job as a part-time volunteer or the highest ranking official in the most prestigious organization. It's a mission of excellence that burns inside of these individuals despite titles or designations.

People who chase promotions check the right boxes, stay late when asked, and typically climb the corporate ladder, rung by rung. Leaders, however, show support for their peers, challenge what has "always been done," and work for the betterment of the team as a whole.

And yes, making your way to the top can potentially come with an impressive salary, but less than 1 percent of people in the U.S. actually find themselves in a CEO or equivalent role. Does this mean less than three hundred thousand working people are leaders? Absolutely not. One could argue Rosa Parks was one of the greatest leaders in history and just a simple factory worker.

A spirit of service will bring you wealth quicker and with greater pride than simply setting your sights on a corner office or impressive title. Gratitude is not found in management, but rather the relationships you build with customers day in and day out. Being committed to your customer is far more rewarding—financially and emotionally—than climbing (often clawing) your way to the top.

**When you change the way
you look at things,
Things you look at
Change!**

Live in a state of forgiveness

And always apologize.

An upset customer is one of your greatest opportunities.

In the time it takes most to complain, you could have sold something.

Time spent complaining at work is time not spent being productive and getting ahead. Yes, venting about irritable co-workers and condescending customers is natural—often commonplace—but it does more than just waste time that could otherwise be spent accomplishing tasks—like selling cars and making money.

Complaining deteriorates workplace culture and creates doubts in the mind of those you work with. If you feel like upper management is incompetent and Bob hears you saying that, Bob may start to question the capabilities of leadership as well—without any other justification. The morale takes a huge nosedive and now you're spending the majority of your day surrounded by miserable, grumpy people. Not a recipe for success.

Likewise, joking to a customer about what a slob your boss is or how cheap your company is doesn't build a rapport—quite the contrary. Customers are turned off by sour comments about the company they are about to hand money to. You may as well tell your customer you think they are idiots to do business with a lousy organization.

The average person spends over fifty-three hours each year complaining. Imagine how many deals you could close given fifty-three hours! Now, imagine the opportunities that will pass you by if you choose to give those same fifty-three hours to moaning and griping about the profession you chose! Yes, some days it's hot—roll up your sleeves and get over it.

You decide—will you keep a positive attitude about your rewarding (sometimes challenging) money-making career or drag into work each day with a gray cloud that will inevitably block you from your full potential?

Progress leads to Happiness and Success!

SUCCESS IN A WORLD OF UNCERTAINTY

Life is about turning points. Some people don't embrace them because they are in fear of change. Over the span of the eight years that I have been in this business, I have learned to view any forks in the road as bifurcate opportunities, turning points that bring positive change from moments of darkness to shifts in a lighter direction.

My main goal here is to encourage you to see change as a means of progression. Anyone can take any start and work to form it into a new ending. When you come to a fork in the road, take it. Always be mindful of the fact that while you cannot change the direction of the wind, you have the ability to adjust your sails accordingly. If you realize at any point in your life that you do not like the direction you're headed in, rather than complaining, change your destination. Commit to this and allow yourself to move forward, fast and true.

Most people are not as accepting to change because they are afraid to fail. When we give ourselves permission to fail, we open ourselves up to excelling in ways we never thought possible. Success is often a matter of moving from failure to failure (because let's face it, that's life) without any loss of enthusiasm. One who fears fear itself limits their prosperous activity. The greatest glory of living life lies not in ever failing, but rather in rising every time we fall. Failure is opportunity. Master your craft.

NO ONE IS YOU, AND THAT IS YOUR POWER

A common quality among salesmen of any breed is an air of confidence. Some people are born with this knowledge of self-worth; others have to work at it a bit, and that's okay. More often than not, acknowledgment of self-worth is brought about by a combination of things. While most people begin with validation, a legitimate salesman needs no validation. They rely on achieving lofty goals to continually advance themselves as well as their positive impact on others.

When interacting with others, especially customers, it is important to let your confidence shine through. A true salesman, from the moment they greet their customer, will walk with steps so large the world will tremble beneath their feet. When they know they've done well, confidence shows that they have the knowledge and power to win others over. Conviction creates an aura that draws people in. Because many people lack high self-esteem, they are generally intrigued by people who have high levels of confidence; they want to learn how these people live their lives, with hope of emulating that energy.

Many aspects of the sales process, especially managing objections, is about transferring that confidence. At the end of the day, it's less about what you say and more about how you are saying it. It's a proven fact that no matter how illogical something may seem, if delivered with enough confidence, people will be receptive to the offer. Take a look at today's politicians—they're a perfect example of this logic at work.

At the end of the day, sales is not a matter of "buy this because it…," it's matching a problem to a solution, whether in the short or long term. How do you uncover a problem? By listening. Be a consultant, of sorts. Be confident in what you are offering; be confident in your knowledge. Be genuinely interested. No person goes to bed at night thinking "I need to buy XYZ tomorrow." They examine all options. Your job is to maintain confidence in self and the product and align their problem with your solution. In the event that your solution is not a perfect fit, they still respect you and your confidence in yourself. You part as friends, perhaps having learned something about each other in the process. Be confident in what you do. Master your craft.

You become something you give yourself. No way out.

You become the boss, the CEO, and the president.

Act like you own the place.

Crafting Success

Success is a dynamic process. It is a potion steeped in failure and ambition. It is also a plan deploying strategy and action. It's not as enigmatic as it seems though. The trick is concocting a formula that works for you.

Check out these ten essentials for success! Which (see what I did there?) did you choose?

1. Initiative

Envision your goal. Decide what it is you want and commit to it. You can't follow a path to success without introducing a clear goal.

2. Passion

An appetite for attainment is essential. Imaginatively feeding that hunger creates charisma. You can't succeed if you aren't enthusiastically pursuing your goal.

3. Precision

Focus on consistency. Credibility and reliability are valuable traits. You can't promote your worth without demonstrating accuracy.

4. Knowledge

Expertise is a no-brainer. Consistently embrace continuing education and ongoing learning opportunities. Don't forget about customer service skills, open-mindedness, and ingenuity.

5. Consistency

A quality performance says it all. Dependability confirms your potential and ability to deliver. You can't expect success without stability.

6. Productivity

Effective actions dominate the workday. Blatant inactivity, along with misdirected energy, is pointless. You can't be successful wasting your capacity or time.

7. Discipline

Embrace the challenge. Balancing self-care and self-destruction can be tough. Success demands self-sacrifice and dedication to your goal.

8. Gratitude

Be thankful for everything. You are exactly where you are supposed to be on this journey. You can't be successful if you don't appreciate the present moment.

9. Loyalty

Recognize teamwork. Influence is all around; build a foundation of resources. You can't find success without honoring those who've gotten you this far.

10. Trust

Integrity produces assurance. Develop a connection with others. You won't attain success without a compatible attitude and honest rapport.

Don't be afraid of success! Pick your poison, mix it up, and master your craft!

Cards are like vehicles that
carry a piece of us into the
hearts of others.
Upon its arrival, it releases
a sort of dopamine into the
brain which puts a smile on the
receiver's heart.

STOP SELLING,
START DATING

The artful dance of pursuing, then securing that first date or first sale have more in common than you might think. On a first date, if all you do is talk about yourself, she may never take your call again. On the other hand, if you sit and listen and rarely divulge information about yourself, you will retain an air of mystery—a modern-day James Bond. This action, in itself, leads to great follow-up; if they don't "buy it," whether literally or figuratively, you will never have that opportunity to continue to build a relationship with that person. But really, there are actually a few other ways the two situations are quite similar.

Making the first move enables you to remove the possibility of awkwardness during the encounter. Whether selling a product or yourself, it never hurts to take a chance and put yourself out there.

Stop trying to be cute. There are so many deals/dates lost when one person tries to progress too quickly, making assumptions and jumping to conclusions. One never makes the first move strictly to gain a new friend. There is no reason to try to come up with some cutesy reason to have done so.

Don't act like you "need it." Whether it is the last day of the month and you haven't hit your goal or you haven't had anything that could pass as a date in three months, no one wants to begin with someone who exudes desperation. You would never ask a girl to marry you on the first date; you never ask for the sale either. You play the game, and they start playing. Even if those details are all you can seem to think of, no one will ever say yes meaningfully just because they feel badly for you.

To really break it down, sales and dating are one and the same. You're selling a product. You act within a marketplace. You develop strategies to accomplish your end goal. Practice your technique and you will master your craft.

Photos are lost online,
but "thank you" cards bring a
smile to the face of the receiver.
This shows that you are caring
about your customer.

INTENTIONAL INFLUENCE – THE ART OF WINNING OTHERS OVER

One of the strongest tools you can have is the ability to reach others and win them over. In any relationship in your life, it is essential to be able to apply the gentle art of persuasion. Don't get me wrong; I'm not talking about manipulation—that is an entirely different beast. It's more about being able to give people reasons to respect you enough so that they want to engage with you and actually listen to your point of view.

By definition, influence is the ability to move a person toward a desired action, usually within the context of a certain goal. One thing that successful politicians, religious leaders, and businessmen all have in common is their focus on how to best benefit those they are influencing with their ideas and what they have to offer, how to express that standpoint Instead of pushing people, pull them in with capable communication skills, tact, and kindness. These small changes will make a huge difference in how your customers see you, and you will always stand out above the others in your field.

Taking pride in building personal relationships with your customers makes business more fun, less stressful, and more profitable. I know that it may not always be so simple. As salespersons, we are constantly met with walls and barriers in the majority of the people we try to reach. Even the most seasoned of sellers may go wrong in their attempt to coerce the people they encounter to come around to their way of thinking in order to push their product, whatever it may be. There really are only a few key points to keep in mind when trying to form a new relationship with a customer:

- **Control your emotions** – Do not let anything that is said or done push you to the point that you become obviously frustrated or backed into a corner. The longer you are able to spend with someone, the more of an opportunity you have to build a positive relationship with them.

- **Understand the clash of belief systems** – People are not always going to agree with everything that you hold to be true. Different people have different ideas and beliefs; that is okay! Just go with it and don't push your views too much, as it will turn your customer off from what you are really trying to show them.

- **Acknowledge ego in others** – The majority of people out there view salesmen as being cocky or overly egotistical. Every person out there has a small bit of that in them whether or not they realize it. Ego can oftentimes intimidate your customers. So instead of emphasizing details in yourself, play off of their confidence and form a relationship with them.

- **Communicate with tact and empathy** – In reality, everyone likes people who listen. People who understand express feelings of concern show that we are important to them.

Quite simply, one of the keys to success is to never be too busy to meet someone new. This is how positive relationships are formed and lifelong customers are made. People buy from people they like. Master your craft.

You will never be successful on someone else's schedule.

You must make your own.

YOU TOO CAN THINK
AND GROW RICH

I'm a major advocate of constant self-improvement, so I spend a lot of my spare time reading and trying to learn all I can to better myself. One of the most influential and empowering books I've read is *Think and Grow Rich* by Napoleon Hill. Written in 1937, the content of this book has managed to retain its relevance even today; the ideas really have stood the test of time. The most successful leaders and business people in the world stand by this book for one reason and one reason alone: **IT WORKS!**

The main theme in this handbook for success is visualization. By definition, visualization is the formation of a mental image of something. The top performers in any industry know the importance of picturing themselves succeeding before they actually do in reality. When you think of things you want to achieve in your life, whether it be a goal or a dream or a wish, most people can't help but think of all the obstacles they may encounter. I know I personally have to step outside of that and stop the obstacles from becoming so big in my mind that I will become satisfied with mediocrity.

Another key to success, and a huge factor in self-betterment, is to allow yourself to learn from others. Whether you reach out to an influential person in your life, or you choose to follow those who inspire you, everyone should take the time to develop a mentor. Learn from their trials and tribulations and apply their first-hand knowledge to your own journey. An outsider's point of view will help you to develop the discipline and perseverance to reach any goal you may have.

If you do one thing for yourself this week, please take the time to get yourself a copy of *Think and Grow Rich* or download a PDF version and get started on it as soon as you can. I promise, you will not regret it.

ALL IN FOR THE WIN – A LESSON IN COMMITMENT

Commitment unlocks the doors of imagination, allows vision, and gives us what we need to turn our dreams into reality. No matter what type of goal you may have set or what idea you have at the forefront of your mind, being committed to that will provide the long-standing push to get what/where you want.

Most people complain about not getting something or about not achieving their goals, about their life being "too difficult." What we need to realize is that the moment you stop the complaints, you come to understand that you don't get what you want in life, you get what you are 100 percent committed to.

To commit to something is to make a clear-cut decision to pursue one path toward your destination. Getting there takes dedication, discipline, patience, and determination to whatever it takes to succeed despite the inconvenience you experience along the way.

When it comes to commitment, it's not solely about striving to achieve the goal itself. It is also as much about the small details as it is about the big picture. Everyone aces small commitments every day; you commit to learning a new skill, to developing a new habit, to completing a task, or even to keeping a promise. How many of these small commitments do you actually keep?

The trick to overcoming the cycle of "noncommitment" is to recognize that there is a difference between a commitment and an interest in something. When you are truly committed to a goal, you are able to develop a clear idea of what lays ahead, the sacrifices you must make, and how to respond to the challenges. Commitment requires clarity. Commit to your calling. Master your craft.

Letters are the most important weapons in a salesman's arsenal.
They must be written with empathy, care, and affection.

LIONS DON'T LOSE SLEEP OVER THE OPINIONS OF SHEEP

In a sales-driven industry, it's sometimes easy for other people to take credit for everything that you have worked so hard to build: your numbers, your customer base, etc. Not everyone realizes quite how hard salespeople have to work. People sometimes overlook the time and effort put into it. As a result, while salespeople have the highest of highs you'll see, we also sometimes encounter the lowest of lows.

I'm proud to say that for the past four years, I've done very well for myself. I have been able to fine-tune my abilities and improve even a little with each day that passes. But that doesn't come without a price. With changes in upper management in any sales-related business, you know that can happen quite frequently. It's easy for others to step in and take the role of "leader" taking credit for the achievements you've worked so hard to accomplish. Some days are better than others. But it gets to the point where you may feel that you're stuck in your own version of the movie, Groundhog Day.

It's sometimes easier to just let circumstances get you down, but there really isn't a lot to maintaining the drive needed to make it far. My secret is that even on the hardest of days, with the lowest of lows, I never lost focus on myself. No one has the power to take that from me. I center myself by really going back to the basics and focusing on my end goal of providing the best product and customer service to each and every person I encounter in my day.

It's not always easy being your own man or woman in today's world. Most people need someone to confide in. Being a leader in this industry means that you are able to work with those above you, still striving to better yourself without overstepping those preset boundaries, the dynamics of the manager/salesman relationship. Your devotion to your job, your "craft," does not mean you ever lose sight of your loyalty to yourself and your ability.

Mirror, mirror on the wall,
why should I sell at all?
So you can become the
richest in the land!

MIRROR, MIRROR

If you can mirror your customer, you really can open your eyes to their soul. The customer will become comfortable and begin to trust you so much that they will welcome you into their lives at the most personal levels. In even the most basic of situations, people buy from people they like.

Mirroring and matching are the simplest of sales techniques based on the concept that people like people most like themselves. You can easily develop a rapport with your customers by:

- Mirroring their body language. This will subconsciously send the positive message that you are paying attention to their communication on every level.

- Mirroring their voice. By matching the pace and volume of their speech, as well as tone and inflection, you will further ensure that you and your customer are on the same wavelength throughout the conversation.

- Mirroring their processing style. Some people are more action-oriented. These customers will want to come in and get right down to business. Others have more of an emotional processing style and will require additional effort from you to develop a rapport stemming from "chitchat" prior to getting to the point at hand. Then there are the ones who have more of an analytical processing style, and they require you giving them hard facts prior to making any sort of decision.

It's important to realize that using these mirroring techniques alone will not guarantee additional sales; they really serve to help make your customer more comfortable with you and with anything you are presenting to them. Add these to your arsenal and you will truly master your craft.

Newsletters can bring two families together. The information shared is personal. This personal connection can be unforgettable in building a lifelong relationship.

A SHOW OF POWER LOOKS THE PART

It's important in a career as a sales representative, especially at a dealership, that you are able to play many roles. Of course, you must look the part to play that specific position. Remember, you want to talk to people as a salesperson, and if that doesn't work, talk to more people.

When a person comes up to you, if you look the part, they may ask, "Are you the manager?" "Are you the finance guy?" "Are you the leasing manager?" My answer is always "YES! YES! YES!" By sitting them down, interviewing them, and making sure you make a connection with them, it will assist you to place them in the right hands. By doing this, you could easily find a sale. I have found much success in playing roles. Of course, there will be times when you really have to get that manager for them, but take them to the desk; as long as they get the help they need, satisfaction will be shown. I've taken freshups and told them I was not a salesman. As they drive away in their new car, they would say, "I thought you were not a salesman," and

I would just smile, beaming my teeth as brightly as possible.

In the auto industry, you will gain much power, although you'll be the boss of nothing. If you become great at what you do, nobody will say anything about what you do! They will revere and respect you for what you do. Remember, everyone is a sale! You've just got to sell them! Of course, it's important that you look and play the part. You've heard it said one thousand times, "Look like you can afford what you sell!"

LETTERS ARE EXTREMELY IMPORTANT

As a salesman, I have many advantages and tools available in today's fast-paced, technology-driven world. With immediate access to communication in various forms and customizable messages, I can contact customers in seconds through email and receive a response just as quickly.

I'M STILL HERE: This is one of my favorite messages to send to clients. I even utilize nonverbal communication and place a hug emoji at the end! Have a good time with your letters and create a relationship with customers. "I'M STILL HERE" is versatile and works for those who made a purchase a year ago or even three years ago.

REFERRAL CHECK: After ninety days, I send established customers a referral check. It looks like a regular check, but at the top I write, "I hope you're enjoying the efficiency of your new car." I write a simple paragraph explaining how the referral programs works. Have fun with this!

GRATEFUL: This message reminds customers that I'm grateful for their time and that I'm here if they need anything. I generally send this out thirty to ninety days after their first visit and thank them for spending time with me whether or not they purchased a vehicle.

LEASING IS PURCHASING: Develop letters that will get people thinking. If a customer is in a lease that is not benefitting them, you may want to show them the advantages of purchasing. Similarly, if they have obtained a loan, you might want to explain the value of switching to a lease.

HOPE ALL IS WELL: This letter demonstrates empathy for your customers. Who knows, maybe there is a global pandemic—ha ha! But, in all seriousness, begin this message by expressing your concern for your customer's family and circumstances. Then follow with your pitch by offering a possible solution to hardships or a positive aspect that has come from present-day situations.

AWARDS: If the cars you're selling win any awards, write a detailed letter describing the category, requirements, and sponsors. Educate buyers, announce offers, and showcase the vehicle. Break it down for customers by illustrating the importance of the awards and whether it is based on safety, innovation design, or performance, for instance.

NEWSLETTER: Create a yearly one-page newsletter consisting of three paragraphs: one paragraph detailing your personal accomplishments (people naturally surround themselves with winners), the second introducing them to your family (talk about your family/children, include a family photo, and let customers into your life) and the third explaining all the personal services that you can extend to them. Sending a newsletter to all past and potential customers will have a giant impact on personal and professional relationships—improving sales and overall interest in your business.

BIRTHDAY CARDS: Send birthday cards to everyone who purchased a vehicle from you. This is a simple reminder that you appreciate your customers and are thinking of them. Sign the card with a sincere greeting in green marker and put your business card inside. This creates another positive connection between you and your customer.

CONGRATULATIONS: This message reminds customers that you understand that they were probably overwhelmed while they were purchasing their new vehicle. While under an adrenaline rush, they might not remember all the details surrounding the features or accessories that came with the vehicle. I send this message out immediately after a purchase. I also include a copy of a survey that I am utilizing to grow my business and a customized newsletter with the headline "Congratulations Michael Lehman" specifying my awards and accolades for the year.

HOW TO USE YOUR PRODUCTS: Send a letter detailing steps on how to use the product. This can be written in a letter, listed in order, or spoken via video (like YouTube or another social media outlet). Get creative with your delivery and methods of teaching customers valuable information.

Throughout the last five years, I have created over 150 letters that hundreds of successful salesmen have utilized and benefitted from. I love to see the excitement on a customer's face when they walk in the door and pull the letter out of their pocket or purse. Frequent communication is essential to the growth of your business. Make these letters creative! Compose them as if you are in the military writing to your mother who you have not seen in six months. Customers will absolutely fall in love with you if they feel the sincerity of your message! Using these tactics, you will become essential to your workplace and become a master of your craft!

Process leads to Progress
through goals.
Remember, other salesmen
will not be willing to
do the work that you are
about to embark on.
Hard work ALWAYS pays off.

Life, Health, and Happiness
(letter from December 2018)

Wow! What a year it has been! I can't believe 2018 is coming to an end! It has been almost nine years now that I have been a part of the American Honda family. In the past nine years, a lot has changed for me! This year, my twenty-three-year old daughter is working in Atlanta in Buckhead. She graduated from the University of Georgia in food science. I am so proud of how hard she has worked to get where she is now! My baby has just turned three. I must say, it was not the terrible twos for me, it's the terrible threes! He has grown so fast it's unbelievable! My wife is still working for Munroe Regional (now Advent Health). She is the director of physician services, and in fact, has just won Director of the Year!! Words cannot describe how incredibly proud I am of my wife. I feel so lucky to have my family, but also to make you a part of it too!

On September 9, I was awarded Council of Sales leadership Gold Master for the second year in a row. Of course, this has taken four years and twelve thousand hours! This has truly taken a toll on me, but of course it is my HONOR to serve and help as many people as I can. I strive to help people reach their goals with where they would like to be with their automotive needs. I want you to remember that I am here for you every single day. You have made me one of Honda's top salesmen and for that I thank you kindly. Believe it or not, you mean the absolute world to me! I have learned so much from all of my customers, and I appreciate every single one of you for teaching me something. I want to thank you for these lessons you have taught me, for they will remain with me the rest of my life. I am actually in the process of writing a book!

Always remember to let me know ahead of time if you are planning to come in to see me. I have built such a big business now, there's generally a line waiting for me every morning! I am here to serve each and every one of you. So please make an appointment with me. I do not wish anyone to be frustrated or waste their day when they have other appointments to get to. Let me know when you would like to come in to see me, and we will take care of all your needs! I do apologize if ever you have been in to see me and I wasn't able to attend to your needs. As I mentioned before, I have gained many customers over the time I have worked here at Honda.

Any time you EVER need service for your vehicle or have any issues at all, you are most welcome to call me on my cell phone. My number is 352-615-8475. Remember, a lot of new guys come through, so just make sure to tell them that you are working with Mike Lehman.

Please remember that you truly mean the world to me and are such a blessing in my life! I will cherish all the memories and lessons I have learned from my customers. You all have added such love and greatness to my life, as well as my family's. I promise to be the best I can possibly be for all of you every day. I look forward to seeing you and your family soon! God Bless!

Health, wealth, love, and happiness!

I pray that these things will bless your family this year! 2019 is going to be big!

I look forward to hearing from you.

Best regards,

MICHAEL LEHMAN

Honda of Ocala

352-615-8475

Dear Friends,

I hope by now you're enjoying the quality and efficiency of your new Honda. I want to remind you that not only did you buy a wonderful car, but you have me here at your disposal as a personal assistant of sorts. Please never hesitate to let me know if there's anything I can do for you whether it be service-related questions, parts, or even just tips on maintaining and keeping your car's performance at its peak. Feel free to contact me personally if you need me. Remember, though, that here I recently created a big business and at times, I can be a little overwhelmed, so please always let me know you're coming.

I now consider you a part of my family; I'm here to help with anything you may need, big or small. May God continue to bless you and your family. And again, thank you for the purchase of your new Honda!

MICHAEL LEHMAN

352-615-8475

Mlegman@hondaofocala.com

USA! USA! USA BUILT!
The 2019 Honda Insight is already bringing in rave reviews!

This is Honda's third generation for the Insight with an upscale interior and decent room for four. This car looks like the Civic, only finer, and outfitted a little bit better. Featuring LED headlights, lane keep assist, brake assist, low-speed follow, driver and passenger side blind spot monitors, also well equipped with USB ports, and all the upgraded equipment.

Take the time to stop by to take a look at this amazing new car! We are sure that it is going to knock the door down! We are also excited because this is Honda's first hybrid built in the USA … THAT'S RIGHT FOLKS, RIGHT HERE IN THE USA! Featuring three driving modes, you will find a very comfortable, quiet, and enjoyable ride! Then, as you pass all the gas stations, you will ride comfortably to the destination of your choice.

We're extremely excited about this new car, and can't wait to see you and show it to you. It has fifteen feet of trunk space, 60/40 folding seats in back and upper trim levels. The sixty-cell ion battery is rated 1.1 kW, the engine is rated 1.7 HP, traction 129. The EPA rating on this car starts at fifty-nine city and forty-nine highway, combined fifty-two miles to the gallon!

I'm so excited about this new Honda product, and would love to spend time with you just to show it. Of course, no pressure! Come enjoy a delicious lunch and have a car wash on me! Please call for an appointment today!

Mike Lehman
352-615-8475
Find me on Facebook!
a.k.a. Batman!

HONDA OF OCALA

Given how many times *Car and Driver* has named the Accord one of its ten best cars (thirty-one times, but who's counting), it should come as no surprise that the 2018 Accord is topping lists all over the place. In its forty-one-year history, the Accord has built a vaunted reputation for quality and for being genuinely fun to drive, all while maintaining its affordability, spaciousness, and comfort. Let's see how the 2018 model compares to the Accords of seasons past.

At first glance, it's easy to see that the people at Honda are starting to realize that taking a safety mechanical approach doesn't quite cut it anymore. This year's Accord takes a more fashionable turn with a slightly greater wheelbase that allows for tighter front and rear overhangs, giving the car a longer and, in turn, more sleek and elegant appearance. While it's normal to think one must trade functionality for good looks, fret not. The masterminds at Honda have found a way to balance it all. The Accord's scooped-out headliner allows plenty of headroom for even the tallest of passengers. In addition, at seventeen cubic feet, this year's model has a trunk that is a full cubic foot larger than the 2017 model.

The base Accord LX trim comes with remote start, a rearview camera, a larger 8.0-inch touch screen, LED low-beam headlights, cloth upholstery, seventeen-inch alloy wheels, Bluetooth connectivity, a 7.0-inch screen, and a USB port. Moving up to the Accord EX trim adds a moonroof, 60/40 split-folding rear seats, Apple CarPlay and Android Auto integration, heated front seats, and an eight-speaker audio system.

The Accord EX-L trim adds a power-operated passenger seat, a ten-speaker audio system, memory function for the driver's seat, a leather-wrapped shift knob, leather upholstery, and an optional navigation system. The range-topping Accord Touring grade adds nineteen-inch alloy wheels, a heads-up display, adaptive dampers, full LED headlights, ventilated and heated front seats, wireless charging, heated rear seats, and parking sensors.

The Accord is a mature sports sedan, tranquil and composed when you want it to be, but ready and willing to play when asked. With a sense of harmony second to none, the Accord engenders confidence.

With that being said, I am offering you an opportunity to come into the dealership and experience the 2018 Honda Accord for yourself. The elegance and class of this year's model, paired with the sportiness that Honda is known for, will leave you wondering how you ever settled for anything less. Please call me directly to make your appointment today.

Best regards,

MICHAEL LEHMAN

Honda of Ocala

(352) 615-8475

Mike Lehman
1800 SW College Road
Ocala, Florida 34471

Thank you and congratulations! I know that soon you will be enjoying the efficiency of your new Honda. After spending hours together trying to buy a car, I myself know it is hard to remember everything we talked about and promises made.

This letter is also to let you know that it is my job to make sure that your Honda's operational costs are very little. Please don't forget to contact me before any services are due or regarding any incidents you may have with the car. Your car will not need its first oil change for five to seven thousand miles.

I want to remind you that the last two years were major years for me in winning Double Gold Status. Only two salesmen have done it in thirty-five years. Now I need your help. This year, I am trying to win Gold Master. Please be gracious enough to give me a perfect score; all tens and yeses, and I will always be here for you.

WHEN HONDA CONTACTS YOU (VIA EMAIL OR PHONE) .... ALL TENS AND YESES PLEASE.

Sincerely,

MIKE LEHMAN
Customer Service Specialist
Find me on Facebook
Add me on Twitter: @carlehman
mlehman@hondaofocala.com
352-615-8475

Honda Survey

1) The dealership staff worked with me to make the purchase experience as timely and efficient as possible. **<u>10</u>**

2) I would recommend Honda of Ocala to my family and friends. **<u>10</u>**

3) The dealership facility was clean and comfortable. **<u>10</u>**

4) I felt the sales consultant understood my needs. **<u>10</u>**

5) The sales consultant was knowledgeable about the vehicle. **<u>10</u>**

6) The business manager completed all the necessary documents in a thorough and efficient manner. **<u>10</u>**

7) The interior of the vehicle was in excellent condition when delivered. **<u>10</u>**

8) The exterior of the vehicle was free of any dents, dings, and scratches when delivered. **<u>10</u>**

9) The vehicle was free of mechanical issues. **<u>10</u>**

10) I received a thorough explanation of vehicle features and technology by someone at the dealership. **<u>10</u>**

11) Someone at the dealership guided me through the following:
   a) Pairing of my compatible phone (s) using Bluetooth* HandsFreeLink* **<u>Yes</u>**
   b) Setting or radio preset **<u>Yes</u>**
   c) Use of audio controls **<u>Yes</u>**
   d) Door lock setting **<u>Yes</u>**

12) The personalized Settings Worksheet was reviewed with me. **<u>Yes</u>**

13) Is there anything you would like to recommend that the dealership do differently to improve the vehicle purchase experience? **<u>Yes</u>**

Ways to Learn How to Use Your New Car

1. Hondatechtutor.com

2. YouTube: "How to use my 2020 (Vehicle)"

3. Owner's manual

4. Your professional salesman.

Always remember: You won't remember everything.
I'll have to see you once or twice more.
Write down all your questions.

I'm still here.

(insert emoji)

You and your family absolutely mean the world to me. I want you to know that I haven't forgotten about you. I am here every day for your automotive needs, not only when you need to buy a car. Also, I can be of service to you and your family for all your vehicle needs.

MICHAEL LEHMAN
mlehman@hondaofocala.com
(352) 615-8475

1. If you need service, call me directly.
2. If you have any problems/accidents with your car, call me directly.
3. Whether you're buying or not, I'm here to serve you.

GRATEFUL

With today's busy schedule, everyone and everything is moving so quickly. I would like for you to realize that I understand how important your time is. So I would like to THANK YOU!

I truly appreciate the time you spent with me gathering information. I am grateful for you. I would like for you to understand I am here for you every day. If you buy a car someplace else, we would like to service it for you here at Honda of Ocala!

Good luck in your search. If you need me, please call me on my private number which I provided on my business card.

Lehman a.k.a. Batman
Honda of Ocala
(352) 867-1900

We hope all is well.

My friend, I hope this letter finds you and your family well. You're constantly in our family's prayers. With all that is going on, we are truly in a learning and growth process.

I wanted to let you know right now is the perfect time to buy, sell, or trade your car. Due to the nation's current situation, some banks are deferring payments as much as ninety days. We are offering as much as $1,000 off select vehicles.

Once again, we hope your current situation is well. Please reach out to me if I can be of any assistance in any way, shape, or form.

MIKE LEHMAN
Honda of Ocala
(352) 615-8475

Overwhelmed

I'd like to once again welcome you to the Honda Family and thank you very much for letting me be of service. Remember, my service doesn't end here. It starts here (at the time of purchase).

With all your busy schedules, time just seems to fly by. Days turn into weeks and weeks turn into months. You may have questions regarding the brand-new vehicle you just purchased. I want to let you know I'm still here.

Remember your VIP parking right by my office. Please remind me ahead of time that you're coming in. Don't forget you mean the world to me and my family. I am a true simple servant; anything I can do for you or your family, please let me know.

Walk confidently toward your dreams
MIKE LEHMAN
(352) 615-8475
Find me on Facebook, Michael Lehman

Leasing vs. Purchasing

I thought I would stop and take a moment to reach out to you. In my position, I am extremely busy. However, from my heart, I'm extremely concerned. After being here for nine years, it's become difficult to reach out to each and every one of you every day. I thought I would take time from my busy schedule, knowing how busy you are as well. Thank you for reading this. I am asking for your advice. The questions at hand are: Are you in the right car? Are you happy with the features?

In today's world, efficiency is a huge factor. I am wondering if you would take the time to contact me to schedule an appointment to be able to answer these questions for you. After nine years, I have never seen a better time to lease or purchase. In most cases, it is just a payment. I have seen them lowered and I've seen people purchase with nothing down. Once again, this is definitely the time.

I want to take a moment to let you know you mean everything to me. Thank you for letting me be of ser-

vice. I look forward to hearing from you so we can improve your circumstances.

Your personal assistant,
MIKE LEHMAN
(352) 615-8475

Dear Friend,

I hope by now you're enjoying the efficiency of your new Honda. I want to remind you, as I told you before, I'm here for you every day. I also want to let you know that we have an *extreme* referral program with a payment of $200. For this program to work, I must know who the customer is before they arrive at the store or before they make any internet contact with the dealership. Generally, when someone buys a car, someone close to them buys a car soon thereafter. So good luck, and please send me all of your friends!

HONDA OF OCALA

Referral Check

Pay to the order of _____ *$200.00*

Two hundred Dollars and no cents ----------

Honda of Ocala

This is not a check

11111111   2222222   33333333333

Respectfully,

Michael Lehman

mlehman@hondaofocala.com

(352) 615-8475

Find me on Facebook!

Michael Lehman:
About Me

The twelfth grade concluded the best four years of my life! After having been voted Least Likely to Succeed (FAILED!), I served eight years in the U.S. Army as a tank driver and eventually became an accomplished NCO trainer while improving my leadership skills (FAILED!). After that, while attempting to adjust to civilian life, I started working for Miller Brewing Company developing new products. I was quickly promoted to sales manager and events coordinator, connecting daily with CEOs and A-list celebrities (FAILED!).

In 1992, I began a business that was mentioned in several articles and turned $5,500 into $1.5 million in sales a month by locating sought-after cars for friends and clients, including athletes and celebrities across the country as well as supplying Ford Motor Company with relevant crash test vehicles for new advancement (FAILED!).

Life took a turn for the worst after the unexpected global financial crash in 2008 and 2009. I lost everything I had worked for and became severely depressed. I remember waking up miserable with an empty bottle and a loaded gun lying beside me. With the taste of metal in my mouth (FAILED!), I made the decision to turn things around and live unrestricted for the rest of my life! Late 2009 introduced new adventures and incredible changes as I joined the sales team of American Honda and helped the company achieve comprehensive revenue goals while building an extensive network of colleagues and customers.

In 2014, after years of hard work, I was honored with membership into Honda's Council of Sales Leadership (COSL) in recognition of sales excellence. I had also earned Gold status, personally selling 266 vehicles, all with perfect client reviews through the Customer Satisfaction Index (CSI). I am blessed to now be known as the 1 percent at Honda for exhibiting constant effort and continuous improvement, ultimately inspiring others to strive for advancement.

In 2016, while operating within the nation's top 2 percent, I won COSL GOLD Master and Top 100, receiving elite status and exclusive invitations to business conventions to expand my goals. As the first to obtain Gold Master status at my dealership in over forty years, and having personally maintained 100 percent positive surveys through CSI, I have had the pleasure of helping Honda of Ocala rank in the top fifteen to twenty CSI in the United States! I am the most awarded salesman that has ever worked at this dealership and consider myself the most personable! I strive to create ever-lasting friendships and professional relationships that promote success for everyone! A #Success is built on determination and opportunity! Find motivation and get inspired on Twitter at #Master Your Craft! #Blessed #Unstoppable.

Just checking on you and your family

Wow, what an epic year this has been! I remember when this virus first hit. I knew it was going to change my life forever. After I regained my focus, I decided to get back to work, and I'm reaching out to let you know how my year is going. This has actually been one of my best years yet. My amazing wife is now pregnant. I don't think I'll ever forget this year with everything that has happened and is currently happening. I bought myself a new Acura because you know I had to go with a Honda. I love my brand! The family is doing well, and most of all, I wanted to reach out and let you know how much you have helped me achieve through all of my seasons.

But most importantly, I wanted to say that I hope that you are all healthy and happy. I want to let you know that I haven't forgotten that you are the reason for my success, a part of my reason why. For this, I am truly grateful. So please ALWAYS remember the following:

1. ALWAYS know that I am here for you on a daily basis. We work hard and sacrifice everything for our customers.

2. ALWAYS remember to call me if you have an accident, if you need service, or if you are looking to buy parts for your car. Reach out to me directly; I will save you money.

3. ALWAYS know that if you are coming in for service, I can set all your appointments by phone. Just call me directly. I can make this easy for you, and I never want you to be frustrated!

To wrap things up, I want to remind you that NOW is the perfect time to purchase a new vehicle. Please tell your friends and family that I am offering a $500 discount to start this process. Thank you for being a part of my Honda family. I am excited to work with you, and I look forward to future possibilities.

WRITTEN FOR FELLOW SALESPEOPLE

THANK YOU AND CONGRATULATIONS!

Thank you and Congratulations! is a three-part letter designed to express empathy and to remind customers that you understand how significant, exciting, and stressful their recent purchase might have been. This letter thanks customers for working with you and indicates your excitement for them as new car owners in a short greeting and then quickly focuses on important information that will benefit you both.

Part one is sincere and practical. You are offering professional advice to protect their investment and their safety. Once the adrenaline from their purchase has lessened, they may need a reminder in the form of a checklist or chart indicating what needs to be done for the optimal performance and regular upkeep of their new vehicle. Reminding customers of responsibilities like routine maintenance, including oil changes and filters for example, will confirm that you care about their purchase. Additionally, remind them that you have offered to help them schedule these services and are willing to help in any way possible. The Thank You and Congratulations! letter reiterates that you intend to build real relationships and do not make meaningless sales.

Part two consists of a copy of the survey that they will receive in their Follow Up letter.

You must explain to them how important the survey is in this business. Their response allows you to evaluate your service and improve your performance in the future. The survey should cover a variety of topics and offer customers the chance to express their satisfaction in a simple, yet detailed format.

Part three is a letter validating your position and purpose. I personally highlight my accomplishments and leadership abilities within the company. I include a letter from the factory commending my performance in the industry as tops in professionalism and sales. This part of the Thank You and Congratulations! letter reassures customers and builds trust in their recent experience with you.

This letter should be charming, supportive, and thorough. Send it out just after customers leave the dealership to remind them that you are there for them and want them to get the most from their purchase. Ultimately, this letter is meant to genuinely thank customers for the time they spent with you and congratulate them on their new vehicle!

FOLLOW-UP

Most salesmen do not realize that the most important customer is not the one looking to buy, but the
one who has already purchased from you. The key to
gaining these customers is enthusiastic and persistent
follow-up. There are many tools that work to demon-
strate your commitment to your customer while reminding them that they are not alone. For these tools
to work, it is essential to exchange phone numbers and
obtain their email address at the conclusion of the sale.
An easy way to accomplish this is to call yourself from
their new car as you are setting up their Bluetooth
connection to quickly get their number into your
phone. Always use the following format to save customer information. JIM AND KELLY SMITH 2021
CIVIC. When your phone rings, you will clearly see
their name and can answer with the greatest line I ever
created, "Hello Jim and Kelly—HOW CAN I MAKE
YOUR LIFE EASIER?!"

Now, to provide customers with your information,
it is best to simply ask for their phone number so you
can add it the way you want it to appear. Always save

your number as the brand you are selling plus your name. For example: HONDA LEHMAN. Just in case they forget your name, this format is clear. It is also great for follow-up because any time they call Honda, they will get you directly.

Over the next few days, text customers to make sure they are easily navigating all their new accessories. Offer another quick lesson (at their convenience) concerning their vehicle's new technology to ensure they are getting the most from their purchase. After they have had a few days to drive their new car, text them and tell them it would make your day to know that they love their car. Make it friendly and fun; add emojis like a gift, smiley, and heart!

Take selfies with customers and their new vehicle—psychology would suggest that both of you appearing in the photo represent trust and family! When they drive away, send the pictures! They will likely use this photo to forward it on to friends and family since it is already in their phone. Now, others have seen you in a photo that resonates trust and friendship, possibly gaining you more customers in the future.

The customer service survey is another great follow-up tool. While initially offering customers a chance to voice their appreciation and satisfaction, it also gives the unique opportunity to contribute ideas and provide reviews. These are tools that you can use to improve your business. In my opinion, there are two basic methods involved in securing a perfect survey:

1. **Earn it!** Treat customers professionally and respectfully!

2. **Beg for it!** Ask customers for help in improving your customer service!

Here is a short example of my survey completion plea to customers:

> ***Good Morning Friends,***
>
> *Lehman here—time for me to ask for your help! My customer service survey was recently sent to your email—please, please provide me with a perfect survey, or I fail! My promise to you is that I will always be available and eager to assist you with anything that brings you back to the store! I am here for you because you are family now! Thanks for being here for me!*

Once you get a perfect survey or an online review, always contact customers to thank them for their time and honesty and let them know how much it means to you!

There is absolutely nothing that tops professionalism and hard work in my field. Most salespeople are not willing to do the extra work, which is the huge fail in the sales business. Some salespeople spend ten to twelve hours in a store, but only work for two hours of them. This is not a physical job. It is a mental game, and you are constantly being watched by the team, audience, and opponents around you! These simple steps may take time, but consistent follow-up is worth the effort!

2020: Challenges, Change, and Encouragement

I'd like to give you my year in review to let you know I'm thinking of you. Wow, where do I begin? As I think back to February when Coronavirus struck the U.S., I remember lying on the couch and crying. I had definitely lost my nerve. Since then, so many crazy things have happened, but you know as humans, we have the ability to adapt, adjust, and continue our progress.

Overall, it's been truly an amazing year. The car business has been flourishing. My amazing wife left Advent Health after eleven years and major stress (to take on a huge position at Heart of Florida Hospitals as director of operations). She seems to be more relaxed and content with this new opportunity. I'm so proud of her for making the move! Our amazing five-year-old son just keeps growing like crazy. He goes to a private school in our area, Corner Stone Academy, and does very well because he loves to learn. He hopes to be an astronaut one day. My older daughter lives in Atlanta,

Georgia and works as a food scientist. I am extremely proud of her.

Getting things back on track, I wanted to let you know that I was thinking of you and the success that you have granted me; it truly means the world! On August 1, I was mentioned as the seventy-seventh top new car salesman in the United States. Let me put this in perspective. There are three thousand car salesmen. I am so thankful for this opportunity. With all of that said, I have three tips for you:

1. ALWAYS: Call me for all your automotive needs or any automotive questions about licensing, titling, or even changing or refinancing.

2. ALWAYS: Remember, I will help you. Please know that sometimes it can be overwhelming with the number of customers I have now after eleven years at Honda of Ocala. So please be patient with me.

3. ALWAYS: Know if you have an accident, if you need service, or if you have general knowledge questions, always remember I'm here for you. Call me directly.

I am offering you $500 off any purchase of a new car. Consider this a coupon, but you must let me know when you walk in the door. Let there be no doubt NOW is the best time of the year to buy a car; don't miss out on this solstice sale opportunity. I look forward to being of service, and once again, thank you for aiding my success brought upon me and granted by you!

MIKE LEIIMAN

(352) 615-8475
Mlehman@hondaofocala.com
Facebook: Michael Lehman

CONGRATULATIONS MIKE LEHMAN!

**Mike Lehman was awarded
Gold Status with
American Honda for 2019!**

**Mike's hard work helped
Honda of Ocala become the
2019 President's Award Winner!**

- **Winner of the Prestigious Honda President's Award**

- **Complimentary First-Year Maintenance** – On every new and used vehicle sold.

- **Free Battery and Alignment Check** – Every time you service your vehicle!

- **Lifetime Car Wash** – Complimentary car washes as long as you own your vehicle!

- **Lifetime Warranty** – On virtually every used vehicle we sell at no additional charge!

- **Price, Payments, and Interest Rate in Under Five Minutes**

- **Ladies Day Every Monday** – Ladies receive a free manicure with any vehicle service.**

- **Three-Day Satisfaction Guarantee** – If you don't love your new or used car, you can return it for a full refund within the first three days.

- **Full-Service Café** – Complimentary breakfast or lunch for all our sales and service customers.*

*Choose from any item on select menu.

** Manicure appointment required.

HONDA OF OCALA

Visit Honda of Ocala Today! (352) 615-8475
Monday to Saturday: 9 a.m. to 8 p.m. • Sunday: 12 p.m. to 6 p.m.

The harder you work, the luckier you get!

JUMP HIGHER

Never remain in an environment where average is accepted. You should make a habit of encircling yourself with ambition and motivation. Your own success will be blocked if you continue to surround yourself with those who are not pursuing it. Live your life to the fullest; imagine the best possible version of yourself and design the best possible future. If you want to build a successful business today, you can either make it happen or you can stop yourself from achieving success. Instead of sabotaging yourself, use roadblocks, obstacles, or negativity as tools to inspire yourself to aim higher. Maybe your feeling trapped at your job, maybe all you want is freedom to live life on your own terms! No, I am not a mind reader, but if you are feeling this way, you are feeling the exact same way I did before I quit my mundane job to become a lucrative entrepreneur. If you need validation, I will be the first to give it to you. I know what it is like to have others tell you that you are about to make the biggest mistake of your life. Typically, they are the ones mistaking determination for recklessness, they simply don't realize that they are making the mistake by not pushing themselves. Promote yourself, encourage yourself, and be your own advocate. You deserve your own support!

IKIGAI
(E-key-guy)

The Japanese word *ikigai* represents a concept that essentially describes a person's passion, purpose, or direction. It is my understanding that the original meaning of this word simply means *a reason to enjoy life*, however there is a more Westernized version in which this term blends what you love, what you are good at, what the world needs, and what you can be paid for. Ikigai can be found within a sport, hobby, activity, or anything that makes a person feel alive, but when a person finds ikigai within their career, they will never feel like their job is work. I know I am incredibly lucky to have found happiness in my career and in every aspect of my life! My enthusiasm for success fuels my work ethic and sales strategies. Finding a productive and rewarding workplace environment should be a top priority, along with setting goals that create a sense of pride and enjoyment. These crucial steps will help pave the way for growth and success in any business. While there are many ways to try to put this into words, *ikigai* is basically a word that encompasses a sense of fulfill-ment or satisfaction surrounding one's purpose in life. I've found mine and would like to help you find yours!

I Just Helped Lehman's
Wife with her Amazon
buying Addiction

Sold!

What is it like to be Married to a Salesman?

I asked my wife to write about what it was like to be married to a salesman, and this is what she wrote:

What is it like to be married to a Salesman? I guess it also depends on the kind of salesman. Can he sell ice to an Eskimo or would even a squirrel not buy a bag of nuts from him? I am married to the Ice Man, so for me being married to a salesman is like living in Florida during hurricane season; Unpredictable and I am always prepared for anything.

I have learned being married to him that there are producers and non-producers. To be a producer you must have the mindset "whatever it takes". As his wife I understand that this mindset does not come with the energy at times to be everything to everyone all the time. It requires focus, commitment, and unwavering dedication to the process. His hours are not set and can change in a moment if he gets a deal. We may have plans, but the plan may have to change. Vacations are scheduled around the month and usually at the end.

Never in the middle. We scheduled our wedding date around the day of the month that was best for him to be off, so patience and understanding is a must. I have learned to take advantage of the quality time rather than worrying about the quantity of time.

There are highs and lows. As his wife I am prepared to support and encourage during the lows and know how to dodge the debris during the highs. I do not mean he throws things; I mean when he is winning he is higher energy than usual and I need to handle it. Whatever "It" may be. Sometimes the highs are more difficult to navigate than the lows because I am naturally a nurturer, so the lows are easy, but sometimes there is the occasional cow that files by and I just adapt.

I have also learned to be "his wife". I try to be what he needs when he needs it, but I am my own person and that is the best. He still cannot figure me out and most days does not remember where I work or what I do, so I just go with it.

The beauty of being married to salesman comes from his success. It can be intense no doubt, but very rewarding when you work as a team. I am his partner, so I signed up for this life. I share in the risks and in the profits. When we profit, I get to go shopping.

Years of chasing the wrong purpose, applying the wrong principles, and seeking the wrong goals taught me that success is not derived simply from money. Success is not an inevitable product of earnings or assets. Instead, success is created in your mind, and it strengthens with a positive mindset. It is entirely possible to manifest the life you want through intense self-discovery and the simple, but powerful belief that you truly deserve the life you desire. Once you actively involve the Law of Attraction in your strategy for success, you will find that sincerely believing in yourself and your ability to accomplish all that you have set out to achieve is your clear path to attainment.

I am beyond grateful for the woman who motivated this awareness. From the moment I saw her, she left me breathless and unknowingly initiated a shift in my thoughts. This incredible woman, who I am lucky enough to call my wife and the mother of our six-year-old son, inspired me to create previously unimaginable success for our family. My wife and son are my reasons for living, loving, dreaming, and creating the life they deserve.

Wholeheartedly believe in the power of attraction and your own potential for success! If you think and live positively, positivity will surround you. If you have a negative outlook, positivity cannot easily break through that barrier. God offers blessings to those who trust his plan and have faith in themselves. My advice is to place your shoes far under your bed at night so that every morning, you remember to drop to your knees and thank God for the life you have and the life you are working toward. As you are planning your future and visualizing your dreams, make sure God is first in formulating success.

May God bless you and your family and may you find inspiration within this small book that leads you to a big life!

Notes

Notes

Notes

Notes

Notes